GW00579049

THE SEA~DYAKS
OF BORNEO

Photo   *G. R. Lambert & Co., Singapore*

A SEA-DYAK IN GALA COSTUME

THE SEA~DYAKS
OF BORNEO

THE REV. EDWIN H. GOMES, M.A.

With a Chapter on

MISSIONARY WORK AMONGST THE DYAKS

by
THE REV. A.F. SHARP, M.A.
FORMERLY ARCHDEACON OF SARAWAK

Opus Publications
Kota Kinabalu
2007

Published by

Opus Publications Sdn. Bhd. (183100-X)
   A913, 9th Floor, Wisma Merdeka Phase 1
   P.O. Box 15566
   88864 Kota Kinabalu, Sabah, Malaysia
   Tel: 088-233098 Fax: 088-240768
   e-mail: info@nhpborneo.com

The Sea-Dyaks of Borneo
by The Rev. Edwin H. Gomes, M.A.

ISBN-10: 983-3987-09-5
ISBN-13: 978-983-3987-09-2

First published 1917 by Society for the Propagation of the Gospel in Foreign Parts, Westminster.

Reprinted 2007 by Opus Publications Sdn. Bhd., Kota Kinabalu

Printed in Malaysia.

CONTENTS.

ILLUSTRATIONS.

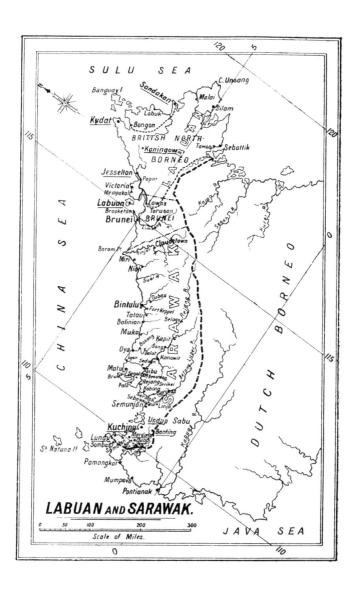

LABUAN AND SARAWAK.

0   50   100   200   300

Scale of Miles.

CHAPTER I.

FAR away in the Eastern Archipelago is the large island of Borneo, inhabited by a variety of races of very different origin, and of various degrees of civilisation. The most important of these are the Dyaks, Malays, and Chinese.

The Dyaks are probably the original inhabitants of the country; the Malays seem to have come into Borneo later, and the Chinese at a comparatively recent date. Most people know something of the Chinese and also of the Malays, but little, as a general rule, is known of the Dyaks. Many, no doubt, have heard of the " Head Hunters of Borneo," and their idea of the Dyak is probably that he is a fierce, cruel ruffian, who spends his whole time in killing his fellow-creatures. But this is by no means the case. It is true that the heads of their enemies are kept as trophies hung up over their fire-places, but it is only in times of warfare that the Dyak shows a thirst for blood. At home and in times of peace, he is a warm-hearted, hospitable, cheery fellow.

There are two distinct races of Dyaks in Borneo— the Sea-Dyaks and the Land-Dyaks. The former live by the sea and on the banks of the rivers. The Land-

I

Dyaks inhabit the interior of the country, and are not so numerous or so energetic as the Sea-Dyaks. The language and traditions of these two divisions of the Dyak race are quite distinct.

The stature of the Dyak is rather greater than that of the Malay, though he is considerably shorter than the average European. The men are well proportioned but slightly built. Their form denotes activity, speed and endurance rather than great strength, and these are the qualities most required by the denizen of the jungle. Their movements are easy and graceful, and their carriage erect. The women are generally smaller than the men. They have neat figures, and are bright, cheerful and good-looking in their youth, but lose their good looks very soon. The women marry at an early age, between fifteen and eighteen.

The colour of their skin varies considerably, not so much between one tribe and another, but in different localities. Generally speaking, those who reside in the interior, on the banks of the upper reaches of the rivers, are fairer than those who live nearer the sea. This may be due to the increase of shade from the old jungle, and the bathing in and drinking of the clear gravelly bedded streams. Their colour varies from a dark bronze to a light brown with a tinge of yellow. Their eyes are black or dark brown, clear and bright, with quick intelligence and good temper. Their mouths are generally ill-shapen and disfigured by excessive chewing of *sireh* and betel-nut. The teeth among some tribes are stained black, and each of the front teeth filed to a point. This is considered by them a mark of beauty!

The Sea-Dyaks are an amiable people and most hospitable. When a stranger walks into a Dyak house, whoever happens to see him spreads out a mat and asks him to sit down. The visitor is then asked if he has had his meal, and if he wishes it, food is given him. In fact a Dyak travelling through the country would not need to take any food with him, as the people of the houses he passed would give him his meals.

The Dyaks are truthful and honest to a remarkable degree, and it is a most unusual thing for them to steal anything. Sometimes in my travels some little thing has been forgotten and left at a Dyak house, but it has always been returned. They are, however, not ashamed to beg, and have no scruples in taking whatever they can get by asking. Their morality before marriage is bad, but when they are married and have children they lead good lives. Adultery is not unknown, but it is comparatively of rare occurrence, and is always looked upon as a crime. They are temperate in food and drink, and gross sensuality is unknown among them. They are, like most Eastern races, apathetic, and show no desire to rise above their present condition.

In dress great alterations have resulted from foreign influence, and the Dyaks who live in or near the towns wear the trousers and coat of civilised races. But the original style still prevails in the up-country villages, and consists of a waist-cloth, generally of cotton, but sometimes made of the soft inner bark of a tree, for the men, and a petticoat, drawn tightly round the waist and reaching to the knee, for the women. Both sexes wear ornaments of brass rings for the arms and legs.

Hoops of rattan, covered with small brass rings, are sometimes worn by the women round their bodies. Necklaces of coloured beads and crescent-shaped ear-rings of a large size are also worn. These ornaments vary among the Dyaks of different districts. Armlets, made from large sea-shells, are very much in favour among some inland tribes. Tattooing is practised by most of the Dyaks. The men wear on the head a bright coloured kerchief, or a small cap made of woven cane. The women have a large sun hat when at work in the rice fields, and at other times wear no head covering.

The custom of betel-chewing is almost universal, and the pouch containing the betel-nut ingredients—betel-nut, pepper-leaf, lime and gambier—is a necessary part of a man's equipment, and hangs round his neck.

The weapons in use are a short, curious-shaped sword, and spears. Bows and arrows are unknown, but their place is partly supplied by the *sumpit*, or blow-pipe, and poisoned darts. The *sumpit* is a round, straight piece of wood about six or seven feet long, through the centre of which a long smooth hole has been bored. The Dyaks show great skill in the boring of this blow-pipe, which is very much used by some of the inland tribes.

The Dyaks live in long houses, in which several families congregate together under the headship of one man. This house is built in a long, straight line, and is raised on posts about ten or more feet from the ground. The floor is made of laths of split palm trees or bamboo, and the walls and the roof are of palm-leaf thatch. Along the whole length of the building there stretches a long verandah, on one side of which is a row of doors.

A SEA-DYAK VILLAGE HOUSE

Each of these doors leads into a separate room, occupied by a family, and serving several purposes. It serves as a kitchen, because in one corner there is a small fire-place, where the food is cooked. It is also a dining-room, because when the food is ready, mats are spread in this room and the inmates eat their meals there. It is also a bedroom, because here they sleep at night. The long verandah is a public place, open to all comers and used as a road by travellers, who climb up the ladder at one end, walk through the whole length of the house, and go down the ladder at the other end. The length of this dwelling varies according to the number of families living in it, and these range from three or four to forty or fifty. From what has been said, it will be seen that a Dyak house is very often a village, though the different families all live under one roof.

It is the custom among the Dyaks to preserve the skulls of their slaughtered enemies as trophies of their success in war. In olden times no young man of any standing would hold a wedding feast without first pro-curing a human head as a present to his bride and as a testimony of his bravery. The possession of one or more human heads was considered necessary before a man could be head of a Dyak house, or be admitted to some of the more important social privileges. Also before the people of a house could give up mourning for their lost relatives and friends, one of their number had to bring home the head of some enemy he had killed. The custom of head-taking, however, is dying out before the influence of civilisation.

In cases of dispute the Sea-Dyaks resort to a trial by

ordeal of a certain kind.   Two champions are chosen to walk into the river, into water up to the waist in depth, in the presence of great crowds of people, and then hold their heads under the water.   The man who becomes unconscious first is defeated, and the party he represents is supposed to be in the wrong.

They plant rice, which is their staple article of food. They grow their own cotton, which they spin and weave for their own use.   They dye it with indigo of their own growing, and with other colours procured from certain roots.

CHAPTER II.

CHILDBIRTH AND CHILDREN.

THE Sea-Dyaks look upon childbirth as a very ordinary event, and there are not many ceremonies connected with the birth of a child, though there are many rules and restrictions which have to be observed by the parents before the child is born.

The Couvade is in existence among the Sea-Dyaks, and there are many superstitions which impede and harass those who are about to become parents. Neither parent may cut anything in the shape of cloth, cotton, etc., nor lay hold of the handle of a knife or chopper, nor bind up anything in a parcel. The husband must under no circumstances tie up anything with a string, as this will hinder his wife's parturition. It is unfortunate if the cord of the water gourd, used by the women, break when carrying water, but in this case evil consequences may be averted if after the accident the woman steps astride over the gourd or other vessel three times, backwards and forwards. Neither parent may eat anything whilst in the act of walking. If the neighbour in the next room should hand anything through the small window in the partition wall, the hand must not be passed through the window, so as to be on the other side in the next room to receive it, but must be kept on its own side of the wall. Nor must either plant a post in the earth, nor dig a trench. Plaiting of basket or mat-work must not be done by the woman. The man may not nail up a wall or fasten together the planks of a boat. No animal, wild or tame, may be killed, whether by trap, spearing or shooting. But should the father be hunting in company with others, he need not allow the wild animal to escape should it come his way, but should he succeed in killing it, all evil effects may be averted from the father or his unborn child by some other member of the hunting party claiming it as his spoil. There are a great many other matters of the same sort forbidden, but in most cases they can easily be avoided. For instance, the mother may do basket-work and make mats, provided some other woman begin the work for her, and the man may dig trenches, or erect a post, or undertake any work of that sort, if the hands of others are first laid to it.

These curious restrictions, more or less similar among the different tribes of Dyaks, are in force until the child cuts its first teeth. It is probable that these restrictions are founded on some theory of sympathy. Man, woman and unborn or newborn babe are all linked together by some unseen bond, and accordingly the wrong action of one may be the cause of bad results to the others.

The naming of the child is not made the occasion for any ceremonies, and it is not unusual to meet children of seven or eight years old who have not yet received a name. They are known by some pet name, *e.g.*, *endun*, little girl, or *igat* or *anggat*, little boy.

Until a civilised government interfered to prevent such atrocious murders, there used to be a custom among the Sea-Dyaks that if the mother died in giving birth to her child, the babe should pay the penalty, and be buried with the mother.   The reasons given by them for this cruel act being that it was the cause of the mother's death and that there was no one to nurse and care for it.   No woman would dare to suckle such an orphan, lest it should bring misfortune upon her own children.   Therefore the poor child was very often placed alive in the coffin with the dead mother, and both were buried together.   This was the old Dyak custom, but it is a long time since it has been carried out to the letter.   I have myself known many cases among the Sea-Dyaks where the mother has died in childbirth and the orphan has been adopted and brought up by some friend or relative.

When the child is born, a fowl is waved over it and then killed and cooked and eaten by the parents of the child and any friends that may be present.

For the first three days the child receives its bath in a wooden vessel in the house, but on the fourth day it is taken to the river.   Some ceremonies attend its first bath in the river.   An old man of some standing, who has been successful in all he has undertaken, is asked to bathe the child.   He wades into the river, holding the child in his arms.   A fowl is killed on the bank, a wing is cut off, and if the child be a boy, this wing is stuck upon a spear, and if a girl, it is fixed to the slip used to pass between the threads in weaving, and this is erected on the bank, and the blood allowed to drop into the stream, as an offering to propitiate the spirits supposed to inhabit the waters, and to insure that, at any rate, no accident by water should at any time happen to the child. The remainder of the fowl is taken back to the house, and cooked and eaten.

At some period after the child's birth—it may be within a few weeks, or it may be deferred for years—a ceremony is gone through in which the gods are invoked to grant the child health and wealth and success. This ceremony is generally postponed till the child is a few years old, if the parents are poor, to enable them to save a little to pay for the entertainment of their friends and relations on the occasion. Where the parents are better off, the ceremony is held a few weeks after the birth of the child. Several Witch Doctors are asked to take part in this performance. A part in the middle of the long open verandah of the Dyak house is screened off by large hand-woven Dyak sheets, and within these the mother sits with the child in her arms. The Medicine Men walk round and round outside singing some incantation. Generally there is a leader who sings by himself for a few minutes, then he pauses, and turns round towards his followers, and they all sing in chorus. Then the leader sings by himself again, and so on. They all walk round, first turning their feet to the right and stamping on the floor, then pausing a moment, and turning their feet to the left, still stamping. This goes on for several hours. When it is over, food is brought out to the assembled guests, and all partake of the provided feast.

This ceremony differs very much according to the

SEA-DYAK GIRL   SEA-DYAK BOY

Photo   *G. R. Lambert & Co., Singapore*

wealth and standing of the parents. Among the poor it is a very quiet affair—two or three Witch Doctors attend, and only the near relatives of the child are present. On the other hand, among those who are richer, this ceremony is made the occasion of holding a great feast, and inviting people from all parts to attend. Pigs and fowls are killed for food. Jars of arrack (a spirit obtained from rice) are brought forward for the guests to drink, and all are invited to rejoice with the parents of the child.

The Sea-Dyaks are very fond of children and treat them very kindly. They rarely, if ever, punish them when naughty, so that they grow up wayward and self-willed. The children as a rule are very fond of their parents, and as they grow older do as they are required from a desire to please them.

There are not many toys which Sea-Dyak children have. The girls often have a roughly carved wooden doll to play with, and the boys are fond of spinning tops which they make for themselves.

The children have very soon to make themselves useful. A little boy of ten or eleven generally accompanies his father in his work and helps him as best he can. A little girl in the same way at an early age helps her mother and learns to do the different kinds of work a woman is expected to do.

CHAPTER III.

MARRIAGE.

AMONG the Dyaks there is practically no ceremony at a betrothal, the young man pays several visits to the lady of his choice, and if the parents of the girl think the match a suitable one, the young people are allowed to see one another very often. On the other hand, if they are opposed to the match, they let the young man know that his visits are not desired, and they do not allow their daughter to see him alone, and the matter goes no farther. Should the parents of the girl place no obstacle in their way, the question of marriage is settled between the two young people to their mutual satisfaction, and the man leaves with the girl some article of apparel—such as his headkerchief, or a ring, or a necklace, as a pledge of his honour, and the two are considered betrothed and bound to marry each other.

The next step in the proceedings is for the man to make known his wishes to his own parents, and then a visit is paid by the man's relatives and friends to the girl's parents to request the hand of their daughter in marriage.

There is a great deal of discussion, sometimes lasting for days, as to where the married couple are to live after the wedding ceremony. The wife does not always leave her home to go and live with her husband, as often as not the man takes up his abode in the house of his wife. Many matters are taken into consideration in deciding where they are to live. If the daughter be an only child her parents generally make it a condition of marriage that the son-in-law come and live with them and work for them, but where the girl has many brothers and sisters they do not insist on that. Then again, the question of social standing comes in, and if a girl marries beneath her she refuses to go to the house of her husband, but expects him to come to her.

When everything has been satisfactorily arranged, and the consent of the girl's parents has been obtained, a day is fixed for the marriage ceremony. The day before the wedding is spent by the bridegroom in obtaining a plentiful supply of betel-nut, *sireh* leaf (a species of pepper), lime, gambier, etc., all concomitants necessary for the guests to chew during the proceedings connected with the marriage.

The principal part of the ceremony among the Sea-Dyaks is the fetching of the bride from her father's to the bridegroom's house. The women-folk of the village house set out in a boat, gaily decorated with an awning of parti-coloured sheets, and with streamers and flags flying, to an accompaniment of gongs and drums and musical instruments to fetch the bride to her future husband's house.

When the boat arrives at the landing stage they all walk up to the house—a gaily dressed crowd, and there they sit down and talk over the future prospects of the young couple, chewing betel-nut and *sirey* the while. A portion of these chewing ingredients are carefully set aside to be used later on ; the Dyak, with his great love for divination, cannot allow such an occasion to pass without some attempt to penetrate into the secrets of the future.

The company all sit down in the long common room of the Dyak house, the betel-nut, *sireh*, etc., specially set aside for the ceremony, are brought forward. A betel-nut is split into seven pieces by one supposed to be lucky in matrimonial matters, and these, together with the other ingredients of the betel-nut mixture, are all put in a little basket, which is bound together with red cloth and laid for a short time upon the open platform adjoining the house.

The person who splits the betel-nut then makes to the assembled guests the declaration that if either party should desert the other for an insufficient reason, the offending party shall be fined to such an amount as has been already agreed upon.

The basket containing the split pieces of pinang or betel-nut is then uncovered, and the contents examined to ascertain the will of the gods. Should the pieces of betel-nut by some mystic power increase in number, the marriage will be an unusually lucky one; but should they decrease, it is a bad omen, and the marriage must be postponed or relinquished altogether. But as a matter of experience they neither increase nor decrease, and this is interpreted in the obvious sense of an ordinary marriage upon which the spirits have pronounced neither good nor bad.

This action gives the name to the marriage ceremony
The Dyaks call marriage *mlah pinang*—"splitting the
betel-nut".

The contents of the little basket, used to discover the
will of the higher powers, are chewed just as other
pinang and *sireh*, and the marriage ceremony is over;
the young couple are lawfully man and wife.

The married couple stay for three days in the house
which is to be their future home. On the fourth day a
visit is paid lasting for three days to the family in the
other village with whom the alliance has been made.
Then the young couple return to settle down in their
new home.

On the occasion of the first visit of the bride to the
house of her husband, she must not enter her mother-
in-law's room until she is led in by that austere relative
herself, or some woman deputed by her to perform that
office. The bride therefore goes into the room of some
female friend she may have in the house, and there
awaits the coming of her mother-in-law, while her
husband sits down on a mat in the open verandah outside his mother's room. The old lady, having ascer-
tained the whereabouts of her daughter-in-law, goes to
fetch her and, having brought her into the room, bids
her sit down on a mat spread for the purpose. Then
she goes out to her son in the verandah and leads
him in and tells him to sit down by his wife's side.
When they are seated side by side, the mother waves
a fowl over her son and daughter-in-law with a
hastily muttered invocation for future health and pros-
perity.

For the wedding and for the subsequent visit which the bride pays to her husband's relatives, she decks herself out in all the finery she possesses and can borrow from her friends. Her wedding dress consists of a short petticoat which reaches to her knees; along the bottom edge of this there are sewn several rows of tinsel and of silver coins, below which probably hang some rows of hawk bells. Round her waist are several coils of brass chain and, in addition, two or three belts made of dollars or other silver coins linked together. From her waist upwards as far as her armpits she wears a corset formed by threading upon a cane a great number of brass rings, arranged so closely together as to completely hide the cane. To this corset may be fixed two or three bands of silver coins. Her armlets of brass or silver extend as far up as her elbow. As many rings as she possesses are on her fingers, and she wears necklaces of small beads, worked in very beautiful patterns and finished off with a tassel of beads, or else a large number of big silver buttons strung together round her neck. Her ears are furnished with studs of silver gilt, with a setting of scarlet cloth behind the filigree work to show them off. Her head is decorated with a towering comb of silver filigree work, to which is attached a number of silver spangles, which glitter with every movement of her head. She wears her hair in a knot, into which are stuck a number of skewers decorated with beads and little tags of red and yellow and white cloth. She does not wear her jacket, though she possesses one; it is slung over her right shoulder.

After this detailed description of the bride's dress, it

Photo   *G. R. Lambert & Co., Singapore*
A SEA-DYAK BRIDE

is disappointing to learn that the bridegroom takes no special pains to ornament his person. The men do wear a great deal of finery when they attend feasts, but on the occasion of his wedding the bridegroom takes no extra trouble about his apparel.

Among the Dyaks no man has more than one wife. Polygamy is considered very displeasing to the gods, and if a man does take to himself two wives, the other people of his village compel him to give one up, and sacrifices are offered to the spirits to avert any evil effects upon them for the crime.

The Sea-Dyaks are very particular as to their prohibitive degrees, and are opposed to the inter-marriage of relatives. The prohibitive degrees are much the same as among Christians.

A man may not marry his first cousin except he perform a special act called *begaput*, to avert evil consequences to the land. The couple adjourn to the water-side, and fill a small earthenware jar with some of their personal ornaments; this they sink in the river, or else, instead of the jar, they fling a matchet and a plate into the river. A pig is then sacrificed on the bank, and its carcase, drained of its blood, is flung in after the jar. The pair are then pushed into the water by their friends, and ordered to bathe together. A joint of bamboo is then filled with the pig's blood, and it is scattered on the ground as the two walk back to the village. They are then free to marry. This ceremony is supposed to avert disaster, and to prevent their own crops and those of the people around from being destroyed by the gods.

CHAPTER IV.

DAILY LIFE—MEN'S WORK—WOMEN'S WORK—
HUNTING—FISHING.

A SEA-DYAK house is really a village in which several
families live under one roof. It consists of a long uncovered verandah stretching along the whole length of
the building. Next to this comes the covered verandah.
On one side of this is a plank wall in which there is a
row of doors, each opening into a separate apartment.
A family occupies one of these rooms. Each private
apartment is furnished with a door which opens outwards
and is closed by means of a weight suspended to a thong
inside. This door can be secured if necessary by a bar.
There is no window to this room, but a portion of the
roof is so constructed that it can be raised a foot or two
by means of a stick, to let out the smoke and to admit
the fresh air. There is no furniture in the room. The
inmates sit on mats, and when they have a meal, the
food is placed before them. Their cups and plates
are hung in rows upon the walls, as much for ornament
as for use. Their valuables, in the shape of old jars
and brass gongs, are ranged on three sides of the room.
In one corner is the fire-place, where the cooking is done.
This one room is occupied by the family, here they cook,

eat, and sleep. The floor is swept after a fashion, but the roof is black with soot from the open fire-place where the cooking is done. This fire-place is made by a frame of lattice-work placed on the floor which is filled with clay. On this there are a few round stones upon which the pots are set for cooking. Above this fire-place there is built a kind of shelf on which the firewood is placed.

Just outside the doors of the separate rooms in a Dyak house is a portion of the verandah about three feet wide, called the *tempuan*. This is paved with wood, and is the part used by travellers passing through the house. Here too the women pound the paddy, in large wooden mortars with wooden pestles, to free it from its husk.

The *ruai* or verandah next to the *tempuan* is open on all sides and stretches the whole length of the house without any partition. It is cooler and not so stuffy as the rooms, and is frequented by both sexes for purposes of conversation or indoor pursuits.

The Dyak houses are clean enough, because all the dirt falls through the interstices of the floor; but the ground underneath is covered with rubbish, and perpetually wet from the water thrown down from the floor above, and being the favourite resort of the pigs and fowls of the long Dyak house, often smells horribly.

The *tanju* or open-air platform is used for drying the paddy in the sun before pounding it. The flooring of this part of the house is generally made of iron-wood, so as to stand exposure to the weather.

Female visitors are usually received in the room, but

male visitors generally sit down in the open verandah, and are not asked into the room unless they want to speak to the women folk or partake of a meal.

The work of the men is to build houses, to make boats and the implements wanted in their work in the fields, and to procure and cut up the firewood. The women fetch the water, pound out the rice, and do the cooking. The women also make their own mats and baskets and weave their own cloth. Such work as can be done in the house is done in the verandah. Here the women weave cloth and make mats, and here the men cut up the firewood, and make the implements needed for their work, and even make boats if not of too large a size.

The Sea-Dyak marries at an early age, and lives in a house of this kind, and does his best to get as much paddy as possible each year. He rises on work-days early in the morning, partakes of his frugal meal of rice and salt, or rice and salt fish, varied if he is very lucky, by a piece of wild pork or venison, which he has received as a gift or bought from some hunting friend. His wife bundles up for him his midday meal in the spathe of a Penang palm, and he goes to his work of cutting down the jungle for planting, returning home late in the evening.

There are days when he does not go to work on his paddy farm, but spends his time in getting firewood, or mending things in his room, or in sitting about in the common verandah chatting with his friends.

The work of planting the paddy [1] is done by the men

[1] Rice in the husk.

Photo

SEA-DYAK GIRLS WEAVING

G. R. Lambert & Co., Singapore

and women together. When the paddy has grown a little and the time of weeding draws near, the family remove to the little hut put up in the paddy farm. In the weeding the Sea-Dyak is helped by his wife, the younger children being left in charge of the elder for the greater part of the day while their parents are at work. When the weeding has been done, the family return to the long Dyak house for about two months. Then they go back to their hut to watch the ripening paddy and guard it against attacks of birds and beasts.

Paddy planting is the chief occupation of every Sea-Dyak, but he has plenty of time for other things, and his life is not quite so monotonous as may be supposed. The actual work of paddy planting and things connected with it, such as the building of farm huts and the getting ready of farming implements, takes up seven or perhaps eight months of the year. The Sea-Dyak has therefore a certain amount of time during which he can visit his friends, make boats, or earn a little extra money by hunting for jungle produce.

The Sea-Dyak women manufacture their own cloth. They plant their own cotton, beat it out with small sticks, and by means of a spinning wheel make their own yarn. This yarn is not so fine as that of English manufacture, but it is stronger and keeps its colour well. At the present time, however, a great deal of the cloth woven by the Dyaks is done with yarn of English manufacture. The warp is arranged in the loom, and the weaver sits on the floor and uses her hands and feet, the latter working treadles. The threads of the woof are then passed backwards and forwards. The work is very slow and Dyak weaving very tedious.

Hunting and Fishing.—The Sea-Dyaks subsist more on a vegetable than an animal diet, so hunting with them is an occasional pursuit, and they fish far more than they hunt. A Dyak village swarms with dogs, but most of these are of no use for the chase, and only prowl about the premises and consume the refuse ood. But some of their dogs, though small in size, aref plucky little animals, and will attack a boar three or four times their size, and not give in until cruelly mauled. Such dogs are of great value to the few Dyaks in each village who care for hunting. Where the dogs are good and know their work, native hunting is not difficult. The master loiters about, and the dogs beat the jungle for themselves, and when they have found a scent, give tongue and soon run the animal to bay. The master knows this by their peculiar bark, hurries to the spot, and spears his game. The boars are sometimes very dangerous when wounded, and turn furiously on the hunter, and unless he is nimble and climbs up some tree near at hand, or is assisted by his dogs, he would fare ill in spite of his sword and spear. The dogs by attacking the hind legs of the boar keep him continually turning round.

Deer are also hunted with dogs and are easily run down upon a hot day. But a more usual way of capturing deer is to find out by following the spoor where the deer rests for the day, and then to hang a *jaring* and drive the deer into it. This *jaring* or net is simply a long cane cable with a continuous series of nooses depending from it and standing five feet high. Two or more lengths are joined together until the required measure is attained. The net is stretched and held in position by light wooden posts. The hunting party then divides, some to watch the net, and others to drive the deer towards it by yelling and shouting. The startled deer spring from their coverts, and make towards the forest, and get entangled in the meshes of the *jaring*. Before they can extricate themselves, they are despatched by the watchers.

Fishing. The Sea-Dyaks have many kinds of seines and nets for fishing in the sea. These are much the same as those used by fishermen all the world over.

Their methods of catching fish in the rivers are worthy of notice. A circular casting net (*jala*), loaded with leaden weights at the circumference and with a spread of anything up to thirty feet, is very much used in the rivers. Great skill is shown by the fishermen in throwing this net over a shoal of fish in such a manner that all the outer edge touches the water simultaneously. The weights cause the edges to sink and close together, and the net is drawn up by a rope attached to its centre, the other end of which is fastened to the wrist of the fisherman. The *jala* can be thrown from the bank or from a boat, and is used both in fresh and salt water.

The scoop-net (*sadak*) stretched on a loop of cane with a handle, is very much used by the women, who are fond of wading in the shallows and scooping up the prawns and fish that come in their way.

The *serangkong* is an open-work basket shaped like

a cone, made of split bamboo or ribs of palm-leaf. It is about two feet in depth, and fifteen inches across the base. There is an opening at the top. It is used by a person wading along the muddy bank of a river, who sinks it in the muddy pools as he walks along. The movement of the fish or prawn inside tells him if anything has been caught, and he passes his hand through the top, and grasps it and transfers it to his boat. The *pemánsai* is a long oval-shaped shallow basket two feet long and woven of cane. It is generally used by the women to catch fish as they wade in the shallow water in some stream or pool in the jungle.

Fishing with hook and line as well as with a spoon-bait is also practised, and there are a variety of fish-traps which the Dyaks set in the rivers and streams.

But the most favourite form of fishing is with the *tuba* root, an account of which is given in the chapter on feasts.

Photo

SEA-DYAKS TUBA FISHING

G. R. Lambert & Co., Singapore

CHAPTER V.

BURIAL RITES.

DEATH to the Dyak does not mean the end of all. He has a belief in a life beyond the grave—a life different indeed in few respects from the existence in the flesh, with all its cares and anxieties—a life with little of the spiritual about it—but still, for all that, life and not annihilation. The soul survives burial and in Hades lives anew, watching his friends on earth, and invoked by them in times of need; and in the Sea-Dyak burial rites there are seen glimpses of a belief in the communion between those on earth and those who have crossed the river of Death, such as we would expect to find only among people of a higher civilisation and a higher education than the Dyaks.

From that distant, unknown land of Death the relatives and friends of the dying man come in a long boat, so the Dyaks say, to take his soul away with them. For a long time there is a conflict between those on earth trying to keep him back, and the unseen spirits urging him to join them. Over and over again, whenever the man loses consciousness, there are distracted cries from those around of "*Pulai! Pulai!*"—"Come back! Come back!"

(25)

As soon as his spirit has departed, the professional mourner sits on a swing near the head of the corpse, and calls upon the different parts of the house, beginning with the roof-ridge and proceeding downwards, and blames them for not keeping back the soul of the dead man. The relatives crowd round and weep over him, and recount, in a loud, pathetic monotone, all his good qualities.

Rice is strewn on the dead man's breast. This is a propitiation to the gods for any wrong he may have committed. According to Dyak ideas, death is the punishment for some sin, and for that sin some sacrifice must be made, or the living may also suffer for it. By sin is meant either the doing of any of the thousand and one things which a Dyak considers forbidden by the gods, or the disregarding of the warnings of birds or dreams. While this sin-offering is being made, others collect his belongings—his clothes, his implements of work, his shield, his spear—which are to be buried with him, and which he is supposed to make use of in Hades. This done, the corpse is carried out to the public part of the house. He is covered with a Dyak sheet, and his belongings are placed beside him. While laid out in this manner, none may step over the corpse. There is no special reason against this, except the general belief that if it were done, the soul of the dead man would not live happily in Hades, but would continually visit his former home and trouble the living.

At sunset a fire is lit by the side of the corpse. All through the long hours of the night the sad watchers sit around, and the loud sustained wailing cry of the professional mourner mingles with the sobs and spasmodic utterances of those who feel most the loss of the dead man.

Early on the following morning food is given him to strengthen him for that long journey to Hades, and a little cotton wool is placed as a pillow for his head. The food is given to the dead in a curious manner. Rice is dashed into his mouth, and the earthen cooking pot is then broken in pieces—it may not be used for the living, having once been used for the dead. The pillow of cotton wool is about the size of a pigeon's egg, and, as far as can be gathered from the Dyaks, it in some way ensures the comfort of the dead man in the other world.

Then the body, wrapped in mats and secured with a light framework of wood, is carried on the shoulders of four men. As they descend the ladder, ashes from the fire burnt near the corpse are thrown after them by the people who are left in the house. This is done so that the dead man may not know his way back to the house, and be unable to trouble his friends afterwards.

When they come to the spot where a tree is to be cut down for the coffin, a halt is made. A fowl is killed and the blood is collected in a cup and mixed with a little water. Each person present is touched with the blood, to propitiate the gods of the infernal world, and to secure immunity from any evil consequences to the persons engaged in the funeral rites. They now set to work to make the coffin. A tree is felled and the required length cut off. This is split in two, and each half is hollowed out. The corpse is then placed inside this rude coffin, the two parts of which are now firmly lashed together with cane.

The procession then moves on. When they reach the spot where the grave is to be, some rice is scattered on the ground. This rice is the price paid to the spirits for the land used for the grave. Then a fowl is killed, and the blood is sprinkled on the ground. These offerings are made to prevent the spirits from hurting any of those who take part in digging the grave.

The coffin is lowered into the grave hurriedly, and all present shout. They cry to the dead man, but why they do so, and what advantage is gained by doing so, is not clear. The reason why the body is hurriedly buried is the fear lest the cry of some sacred bird may be heard and the burial of the man become unpropitious ; the less time they take in putting the corpse into the grave, the less chance there is of this.

Those who leave the grave last plant in the path a few sticks slanting towards the grave, so that no spirits from Hades may follow them—the sticks planted in the ground being supposed to prevent their doing so. All this is done in great haste, because if the cry of any sacred bird is heard before the spot where the coffin was made is reached, dreadful consequences may follow. When this spot is reached, a halt is made. The blood of the fowl killed there before the coffin was made is divided, and each man takes some of it home and touches with it those in the house who were not present at the funeral.

At sunset a fire is lit at the landing-place on the bank

of the river, near the house of the dead man. This fire
is kept burning all night.

On the third day after the death a feast is given, all
the families in the long Dyak house helping to supply
food for the guests who are invited from the villages
around. A plate containing rice and other eatables, as
well as a Dyak chopper, an axe, and a cup are taken
by a large company to the room of the dead man.
They go with much shouting to tell the mourners to
weep no more, and to give the dead man food. They
enter the room, and one of them—generally an old
man of some standing—pushes open the window with
the chopper, and the offering of food is thrown out for
the benefit of the dead man and his spirit friends. As
soon as this is done, men and women busy themselves
in arranging the food for the assembled guests. Up to
this time the relatives of the dead live in strict seclusion,
but after it, they may come out to the public part of
the house, and return to their usual occupations.

But the dead man is not forgotten. Periodical
mournings, at intervals of two or three months, are
held in honour of him, and the professional mourner
calls upon him and weeps over him. The Dyaks believe
that the dead hear their cries, and that a bond of
sympathy unites them with those on earth.

A year or more after the death, a feast is held, and
small baskets supposed to represent the different implements a man or woman uses in work when alive, are
made and placed on the grave. Thus they furnish the
dead man with the means of livelihood in Hades.
This feast ends all mourning for the dead, and after

it has been held, no more periodical mournings are held in honour of him.

But even after all mourning has ceased, the Dyak still believes that his dead friends and relations live and visit the earth. Before going forth on an expedition against the enemy, the dead are invoked and are begged to help their friends on earth, so that they may be successful against their foes. In times of peril and of need, the dead are called upon. And on the hilltops or in the solitudes of the jungle, a man often goes by himself and spends the night in the hope that the spirit of some dead relative may visit him, and in a dream tell him of some charm by means of which he may overcome difficulties and become rich and great.

Photo   *G. R. Lambert & Co., Singapore*

SEA-DYAKS RETURNING FROM TUBA FISHING

CHAPTER VI.

OMENS.

THE Dyak is conscious of his ignorance of the natural laws which govern the world in which he lives. He longs for some guidance in his precarious farming, in his occupations in the lonely depths of the jungle, in his boating over the dangerous rapids or treacherous tides of the swift rivers. He is aware that death and destruction may suddenly confront him from many a hidden source. He knows that Nature has voices, many and wondrous, and he is convinced that if he could only understand those voices aright he would know when to advance and when to recede. He feels the need of guidance, and he has devised for himself a system of omens.

Like the ancient Romans, who took auguries from the flight or notes of certain birds—the raven, the owl, the magpie, the eagle and the vulture—the Dyak has his sacred birds, whose flight or calls are supposed to intimate to him the will of unseen powers. They are seven in number, and their native names are— *katupong, beragai, kutok, embuas, nendak, papua* and *bejampong.* They are beautiful in plumage, but, like most tropical birds, they have little song and their calls are shrill and piercing. They are supposed to be personifications and manifestations of the seven spirit sons of the great god *Singalang Burong.*

It is not only to the cry of birds that the Dyaks pay heed. There are certain animals—the deer, the armadillo, the lizard, the bat, the python, the cobra, even the rat, as well as certain insects—all of which may be omens under certain circumstances. But these other creatures are subordinate to the birds, from which alone augury is sought at the beginning of any important undertaking. The system, as carried out by the Dyaks, is very elaborate and complicated. Some idea of it may be gathered from what is done at the commencement of the yearly rice-farming. Some man, who has the reputation of being fortunate and has had large paddy crops, will be the augur, and undertake to obtain omens for a large area of land, on which he, as well as others, intends to plant. The Dyaks begin clearing the ground of jungle and high grass when the Pleiades appear at a certain height above the horizon at sunset. Some little time before this the augur sets about his work. He will have to hear the cry of the *nendak,* the *katupong* and the *beragai,* all on his left. If these cries come from birds on his right, they are not propitious. The cries of the other sacred birds must sound on his right. He goes forth in the early morning and wanders about the jungle till the cry of the *nendak* is heard on his left. He will then break off a twig of anything growing near, and take it home, and put it in a safe place. But it may happen that some other omen bird or animal is first to be seen or heard. In that case he must give the matter up, return, and try his chance another day. Thus sometimes several days pass before he has obtained his first omen. When he has heard the *nendak*, he will then listen for the *katupong* and the other birds in the necessary order. There is always the liability of delays caused by the wrong bird being heard, and it may possibly be a month or more before he obtains all those augural predictions which will give him confidence in the success of his labours. The augur has now the same number of twigs as birds he has heard. He takes these to the land selected for farming, buries them in the ground, and with a short form of address to the birds and to *Pulang Gana*—the god of the Earth—clears a small portion of the ground of grass or jungle, and then returns home. The magic virtues of the birds have been conveyed to the land, and the work of clearing it for planting may be begun at any time.

The sacred birds can be bad omens as well as good. If heard on the wrong side, or if in the wrong order, the matter in hand must be postponed or altogether abandoned, unless a subsequent conjunction of good omens occurs, which in the judgment of old experts, more than counterbalances the bad omens.

I have mentioned the omens necessary before planting the seed. In a similar manner, before beginning to build a house, or starting on a war expedition, or undertaking any new line of action, certain omens are required if good fortune is to attend them, and the fates are to be propitious.

But it is not only at the commencement of an undertaking that omens are sought. The continuance of good fortune necessitates the observance of omen influence at all times and in all places.

With regard to farming, where the practice is most conspicuous, if any of these omen birds are heard or seen by the Dyak on his way to his paddy lands, it either foretells good or evil to himself or to his farm. If the former, then all is well, and he goes on his way rejoicing; if the latter, he will at once turn back and wait for the following day before proceeding again. The *nendak* foretells good, whether heard on the right hand side or the left, but the *papua* is of evil omen, and if heard, the man must at once beat a retreat.

When a remarkably good omen is heard—one which foretells a plentiful harvest—the man must go to his farm at once, and do some trifling work there and then return, and in this way clench the foreshadowed luck, and at the same time reverence the spirit which promises it.

But the worst of all omens is to find anywhere on the farm the dead body of any animal, especially if it be that of any included in the omen list. It infuses a deadly poison into the whole crop, which is sure to kill one or other of the owner's family within the year. When such a terrible thing happens, they test the omen by killing a pig, and divining from the appearance of the liver immediately after death. If the liver is pronounced to be of good omen, then all is well, but if not, then all the rice grown on that ground must be sold.

Other people may eat it, for the omen only affects those who own the crop.

The Dyak pays heed to these omen creatures, not only in his farming, but in all his journeyings and in any kind of work he may be doing. If he be going to visit a friend, the cry of a bird of ill-omen will send him back. If he be engaged in carrying beams from the jungle for his house, and hear a *kutok*, or a *bejampong*, or an *embuas*, he will at once throw down the piece of timber, and it will be left there for a day or two, or perhaps abandoned altogether. If at night the inhabitants of a long Dyak house hear an owl make a peculiar noise called *sabut*, they will all hastily leave the house in the early morning, and remain away some weeks, living in temporary sheds, and only return to the house when they hear a *nendak* or a *beragai* on their left. There are many omens which make a place unfit for habitation, and among them are a *beragai* flying over the house, or an armadillo crawling up into it.

There are other creatures besides birds whose warnings the Dyaks observe. A cobra or rat crossing the path means that the advancing party must return. A deer crying near a farm prevents the people from doing any work that day. The cry of certain insects—the *rioh*, the *rejah*, the *burong malam*—are also omens which foretell evil.

To kill one of these omen creatures—be it bird or insect—is a crime sure to be punished by sickness or death. But this idea of sacredness of life, it may be noticed, does not apply to the deer, the gazelle, the mouse-deer, the armadillo and the iguana, all of which they freely kill for food. Rats also are killed, as they are great pests. It would seem that physical wants are stronger than religious theory. Another inconsistency appears when, in setting up the posts and framework of a new house, they beat gongs and make a deafening noise to prevent any bird of ill-omen being heard.

This is the merest outline of the practice of omens among the Dyaks, but it will give some idea of the tediousness of the system. And the intricacies of the subject are great. The different combinations of these voices of Nature are endless, and it is difficult to know in each special case whether the spirits intend to foretell good or bad fortune. It is not at all an unusual thing to see old men sitting down for hours discussing the probable effect of some special combination of omens upon their destiny.

A favourite way of auguring good or evil among the Dyaks is the old classical method of examining the entrails of some animal offered in sacrifice. A pig is killed, and the heart and liver taken out and placed upon leaves. These are handed round to old men present, who closely examine them, and pronounce them to be either of good or bad omen. This method of augury is often resorted to when it is doubtful what the omens from the cries of birds may mean.

A study of the subject of omens and augury shows the need the Dyak feels, in common with all mankind, of some guidance from higher and unseen powers. What is the principle which underlies this system of omens? There is no doubt a morbid anxiety to know the se-

Photo   *G. R. Lambert & Co., Singapore*

A SEA-DYAK CHIEF

crets of the future.   But that is not all.   Surely, in
addition to this, there is the hidden conviction that the
gods have some way of revealing their wishes to mankind, and that obedience to the will of the higher powers
is the only way to ensure success and happiness.

CHAPTER VII.

MOST races of mankind believe in the existence of a class of beings intermediate between deity and humanity. The Dyak is no exception, and he believes that innumerable spirits or *antu* inhabit the forests, the rivers, the earth and the heavens; but whereas among other races the spirits seem to act as mediators between the gods and mankind, this is not the case among the Dyaks, because they believe that their gods actually give their presence in answer to invocations and sacrifices, so that the distinction between spirits—*antu*—and gods—*petara* —is among them a little vague. There are both good and evil spirits: the former assist man, the latter do him injury. Of the gods no evil is predicted, and so it comes to pass that the good spirits are nearly identical with their gods.

Any unusual noise or motion in the jungle—anything which suggests to the mind some invisible operation, is at once attributed by the Dyak to some spirit, unseen by human eyes, but full of mighty power. Though generally unseen, these spirits sometimes vouchsafe to mankind a manifestation of themselves. When they do so, the form they assume is not anything very supernatural,

(38)

but either a commonplace human form or else some animal, a bird or a monkey, such as is often seen in the forests. There is, however, the Chief of the Evil Spirits, Girgasi by name, who, when seen, takes the form of a giant about three times the size of a man, is covered with rough shaggy hair, and has eyes as big as saucers, and huge glittering teeth.

The spirits rove about the jungle, and hunt for wild beasts like the Dyaks do themselves. Girgasi, who, when seen, assumes a most formidable appearance, is specially addicted to the chase, and is often to be met with hunting in the forest. There are certain animals which roam about in herds in the jungle, and are called by the Dyaks *pasan*. These are supposed to be the dogs of the spirits when they are out hunting, and they attack those whom the spirits wish to kill. I have never seen one of these animals, but, to judge from the description of them, they seem to be a kind of small jackal. They will follow and bark at men, and from their supposed connection with the spirits are greatly feared by the Dyaks, who generally run away from them as fast as they can.

There are innumerable stories told by the Dyaks of their meeting with spirits in the jungle, and sometimes speaking to them. Such stories generally relate how the man who sees the spirit rushes to catch him by the leg—he cannot reach higher—in order to get something from him, but he is generally foiled in his attempt, as the spirit suddenly vanishes. But some men, it is believed, do obtain these much coveted gifts, and if a Dyak gets a good harvest of paddy it is attributed to

some magic charm that he has received from some
kindly spirit. So also, if he be successful on the warpath, he is credited by his fellows with the succour of
some mysterious being from the spirit world.

A Dyak in Banting solemnly told me that one day
when out hunting he met a spirit in human form sitting
on a fallen tree. Nothing daunted, he went and sat upon
the same tree, and entered into conversation with him,
and asked him to give him some charm. The spirit
gave him some magic medicine which would, by the
mere fact of its possession by him, give his dogs pluck
to attack any wild pig or deer. Having given him this,
the spirit advised the man to return quickly, for his dogs,
he said, would be back soon and might do him harm.
This advice he willingly followed, and hurried away as
fast as he could!

Medicines for the sick are believed to be given in
dreams, and many a Dyak relates how, when despaired
of by all, some kind spirit gave him in his sleep some
charm, by the magic virtue of which he was completely
cured. Sometimes when these spirits bestow these
gifts—bits of stick or pebbles or other rubbish—they
also mention the price to be paid for them by others
who need them. There is plenty of room here for the
play of self-interest and trickery; but the fact that such
strange beliefs are acted upon is evidence of a true faith
in them.

The spirits are said to build their invisible habitations
in trees, and many trees are considered sacred as being
the abode of a spirit or spirits, and to cut one of these
down would provoke the spirit's vengeance.

The tops of hills are considered favourite haunts of the spirits, and when Dyaks fell the jungle for planting on the larger hills, they often leave a clump of trees on the summit as a refuge for them.

According to Dyak belief, the evil spirits by far out-number the good ones. All evil is attributed to some *antu* or spirit; every sickness is the result of a blow from some unseen foe. The usual answer one receives when asking what is the matter with a sick man is "*Pansa utai*," "something passed him," that is to say, "a spirit passed him and inflicted the malady". Any serious epidemic is caused by the devastating pre-sence of a powerful and revengeful spirit. Small-pox is called "*Sakit Rajah*," "the disease of the king," that is to say, "the disease inflicted by the king of evil spirits". Cholera is caused by some malicious spirit from the sea, who wishes to kill and eat human victims.

There are many strange customs connected with the Dyak belief in spirits. As all illnesses are caused by the spirits, it is necessary that these be propitiated. When a man is ill the medicine men are called in, and they walk round and round the sick man, and make in-cantations to the spirits and beseech them to spare his life and make him well. When there is any great epi-demic in the country—when cholera or small-pox is killing its hundreds on all sides—one often notices little offerings of food hung about, animals killed in sacri-fice, and blood splashed about. When one asks why all this is done, they say they do it in the hope that when the evil spirit, who is thirsting for human lives, comes along and sees the offerings they have made and the animals killed in sacrifice, he will be satisfied with those things, and not take the lives of any of the people in the house.

As a matter of fact, this making of sacrifices to the evil spirits is a frequently recurring feature in Dyak life. The gods are good and will not injure them, and so the Dyaks worship them at their own convenience, when they wish to obtain any special favour from them. But the evil spirits are always ready to do them harm, and to take the lives of victims, and therefore sacrifices must constantly be made to the spirits, who will accept sacrificial food in substitution for the lives of human beings.

The longing to communicate with the supernatural is common to all. The Dyak has a special means of bringing this about; he has a custom which is called "nampok". To "nampok" is to sleep on the top of some mountain in the hope of meeting some good spirit from the unseen world. A man who is fired with great ambition to shine in deeds of strength and bravery, or who desires to attain the position of a chief, or to be cured of an obstinate disease, will sometimes spend a night, or nights, by himself on a lonely mountain, hoping to meet some benevolent spirit who will give him what he desires. To be absolutely alone is a primary condition. It can easily be understood how the desire would in many cases bring about its own fulfilment. The earnest wish acting upon a lively and superstitious imagination in the solemn solitude of the jungle would probably make the man dream of some spirit or mythic hero.

The Dyak has no temple erected in honour of some god to which, like the ancients of the Western World, he can make a pilgrimage. He has no altar before which he can spend the night in order to receive revelations in dreams, but he goes instead to the lonely mountain top and makes his offering, and lies to rest beside it. The spirit and the object in both cases are the same. The story often told of a miraculous cure is also similar in each case.

CHAPTER VIII.

THE three principal religious feasts of the Sea-Dyaks are connected with Head-hunting, Farming, and the Dead. They are called, respectively, the Bird Feast, the Stone Feast, and the Spirit Feast.

Though these three feasts differ in their aims, there is a great deal which seems to be common to them all. The social character of all these feasts seems to be of more importance than the religious aspect, and the feasting of the guests is of more importance than any offerings made to the spirits or gods. In none of these feasts does there seem to be any real reverential religious worship. It is true food is offered to the spirits, but this is done as the mere observance of an ancient custom, without any approach to religious reverence. There are also long incantations made to the higher powers by men selected for that purpose, who have good memories and can recite in a monotonous chant the special hymns of great length connected with each feast. But the guests do not share in it as in an act of religious worship. They are generally sitting round, talking and laughing and eating. While these incantations are sung, topics of common interest are discussed

(44)

Pho'o   G. R. Lambert & Co., Singapore

A SEA-DYAK YOUTH

and plans formed, and in all these feasts, sociability, friendship, and the partaking of food and drink seem to take a more prominent place than any religious worship.

The preparations for all these feasts are much alike. They extend over a length of time, and consist for the most part in the procuring of food for the guests. The young men go round to their friends, far and near, and obtain from them presents of pigs or fowls for the feast, and as cock-fighting is loved by the Dyaks, they at the same time procure as many fighting cocks as possible.

Before the date fixed for the feast, a great *tuba*-fishing takes place, when the juice of the *tuba* root (*Cocculus indicus*) is put into the water of some river to poison it and cause the fish to rise stupefied to the surface. All the people of the long Dyak house— men, women, and children—accompanied by their friends, go to some river which has been previously decided upon. A fence, made by planting small posts closely together in the bed of the river, is erected from bank to bank. In the middle of this fence there is an opening leading into a square enclosure made in the same fashion, into which the fish enter, in trying to escape from the *tuba* into fresh water. The canoes then proceed several hours' journey up river, until they get to the place decided on beforehand, where they stop for the night in small booths which they put up on the banks of the river. The small boats are then cleared of everything in them, and got ready for use the next day.

Most of the people bring with them some *tuba* root, made up into small close bundles the thickness of a man's wrist, and about six inches long. Early the next morning, some of the canoes are filled with water, and the root is beaten and dipped into it. For an hour or so, fifty or more clubs beat a lively tattoo on the root bundles, as they are held to the sides of the boats. The *tuba* is dipped into the water in the boat and wrung out from time to time. This gives the water a white frothy appearance like soapsuds. The Dyaks, armed with fish-spears and hand-nets, wait in readiness in their canoes. At a given signal the poisoned liquid is bailed out into the stream, and the canoes, after a short pause, begin to drift slowly down the current. The fish are stupefied, and as they rise to the surface, are speared by the Dyaks, who stand up in the bows of their canoes. The large fish are thus secured amid much excitement. The women and children join in the sport, and scoop up the smaller fish with hand-nets. The *tuba* does not seem to affect the flesh of the fish, which can be cooked and eaten.

This favourite form of fishing is always a great event among the Dyaks, because besides the large amount of fish procured, there is a great deal of fun and excitement, and it is looked upon as a pleasant sort of picnic.

Anybody, whether contributors of *tuba* or not, may join in the sport of getting the fish, either by means of spears or hand-nets. But, as is only just and fair, the fish caught in the enclosure near the mouth of the stream is divided among those who have supplied the *tuba* for the day's fun.

The special characteristics and religious aspect of each of these feasts must now be noticed.

THE BIRD FEAST.—This is the most important of all feasts.   It is also called the *Head Feast*, because part of the ceremony connected with it is the giving of food to some human heads taken in war.   In the old days this feast was only held on the return from a war expedition in honour of the heads of the enemy brought home in triumph.   But in the present day this feast is organised when they get a good harvest and the people of a Dyak's house seem so inclined, and if no new heads have been lately brought home as trophies, some old smoked heads that have been in the house for years are used.

A large figure of the rhinoceros hornbill is previously carved in wood, and at this feast it is first of all *timanged* or sung to in a monotonous manner.   This is looked upon as a kind of consecration of it.   Then this wooden figure—called *Tenyalang* by the Dyaks—is set on a high pole which is fixed into the ground in front of the house.   An offering of Dyak delicacies is hung up under it for its food.

This feast is given in honour of Singalang Burong, who is a great and powerful spirit, the god of war and the inspirer of bravery.   When seen, he takes the form of the white and brown hawk so common in Borneo. Why the *Tenyalang* should represent the rhinoceros hornbill and not the hawk is an inconsistency for which there seems to be no explanation.

Some human heads are placed in large brass dishes in the verandah, and to these offerings of food and drink

are made. There are also certain erections called
padong put up at regular intervals in the long verandah
of the Dyak house, and to these are hung war-charms,
and swords and spears, etc. Then the performers walk
up and down, going round the *padong* and the heads
in the brass dishes, singing the Mengap or song of the
Head Feast. There are generally two principal singers,
each of whom is followed by five or six others. The
leaders sing in turn a few lines, and the rest join in the
chorus at the end of each verse. They all hold long
walking sticks in their hands, and stamp their feet as
they walk along.

This song takes the form of a story setting forth how
the mythical hero, Klieng, held a Head Feast on his
return from the warpath, and invited the god of war,
Singalang Burong, to attend it. It describes at great
length all that happened on that occasion. The singing
of this song takes a whole night. It begins at 7 P.M.
and lasts till the next morning. Except for a short
interval of half an hour for rest in the middle of the
night, the performers are singing all the time. The
killing of a pig and examining the liver to find out
whether good or bad fortune is in store for them, is the
last act of the ceremony.

GAWAI BATU—THE STONE FEAST.—This feast
takes place before the farming operations begin, and
is in honour of Pulang Gana, the god of the land, who
lives in the bowels of the earth, and has the power
to make the land fruitful or unfruitful. In this feast
invocations are made to Pulang Gana, and he is asked
to give them a good harvest. The whetstones are also

placed in a heap in the verandah of the Dyak house, and offerings are made to them with a request that they may sharpen their farming implements, and thus lighten their labours. After the feast is over, the whetstones are taken to the different farms, and the work of cutting down the jungle for planting begins.

GAWAI ANTU—THE SPIRIT FEAST.—This is a feast given in honour of the dead. No definite time is fixed for it, and it occurs at intervals of from one to three years.

The preparations for this feast consists in getting ready wooden memorial monuments for the graves of the dead. The women weave with finely split bamboo small imitations of various articles of personal and domestic use, and these are afterwards hung over the grave, and are given to the dead for their use in the other world. If it be a male, a bamboo gun, a shield, a war-cap, a bag for the chewing ingredients, a drinking vessel, etc., are woven; if a female, a loom, a fishing basket, a winnowing fan, and other things; if a child, bamboo toys of various descriptions.

In the evening comes the formal putting off of mourning. The rattan tying up the bundle containing the finery and ornaments of the people who are in mourning is cut by some old man, and the owners put on their bright garments and resume the use of personal ornaments.

The professional wailer sits on a swing in the verandah, and in a monotonous song invites all the spirits of the dead to attend this feast given in their honour.

The morning after the feast, the monuments, the bamboo imitation articles, and the cast-off mourning garments, are taken and arranged on the graves. This is the last duty to the dead, and after this final equipment the dead relinquish all claims on the living.

To all these feasts the whole neighbourhood for miles around are invited. Some weeks before the day appointed, small parties of three or four are despatched in different directions, and these go from house to house and invite the people to the feast.

The men and women come to a feast dressed in the brightest colours, and wearing many ornaments, and the whole assembly has a very gay appearance. For amusements, they have dancing, cock-fighting, and trials of strength among the young men. There are two kinds of dancing—the *Mencha* or Sword-dance, and the *Ajat* or War-dance. In the former, two swords are placed on the mat, and two men begin slowly from the opposite ends turning their bodies about, extending the arms and lifting the legs in grotesque but not un-graceful attitudes. After moving around for some minutes, they seize the swords and they pass and repass each other, now cutting, now crossing swords, retiring and advancing. The *Ajat* is danced by one man, and he acts in pantomime what is done when on the warpath. The dancer begins by imitating the creeping through the jungle in a cautious manner. The lurking enemy is suddenly discovered, and after some rapid attack and defence, a sudden plunge is made upon him, and he lies dead on the ground. The taking of the head of this invisible enemy in pantomime now follows.

Photo   G. R. Lambert & Co., Singapore

SEA-DYAK GIRL IN GALA COSTUME

Both kinds of dancing are accompanied by the striking of brass gongs and drums.

Cock-fighting is a favourite amusement among the Dyaks, and there is a great deal of it at all Dyak feasts. They tie on artificial steel spurs to the fighting cocks, and a bird is cut in pieces and killed in a very short time.

Besides wrestling, there are other trials of strength among the Dyaks. Sometimes two youths sit on a mat opposite each other, foot being placed against foot, and a stout stick is grasped by both their hands. Each then throws himself back, so as to raise his adversary from the ground.

At all Dyak feasts there is a great deal of eating and drinking. Besides rice and meat and fish and vegetables, there are different kinds of cakes handed round to the guests. Their drink is *tuak*, a spirit which they themselves obtain from rice. A great deal of this is consumed, and it is the usual thing to see a great deal of drunkenness at a Dyak feast. If none of the guests were intoxicated, the hosts would be considered niggardly and wanting in hospitality. It must not be supposed, however, that the Dyaks are habitual drinkers ; on the contrary, except at feasts, they are very sober people.

CHAPTER IX.

THE WITCH DOCTOR OR MANANG AMONG THE DYAKS.

AMONG the lower races of mankind there is always to be found the Witch Doctor, who claims to have mysterious powers and to be able to hold communication with the Spirit World. Where there is ignorance as to the cause of disease and the effects that different medicines have on the human frame, magical ceremonies and pretensions to supernatural powers are allowed full sway. Fear and anxiety in cases of sickness make men eager to believe in any suggested means of cure, however absurd they may be. The Dyaks are no exception to the rule. They have their Manangs or Witch Doctors.

The Manang is an important person among the Dyaks, and is summoned in all cases of serious illness. He alone is supposed to wield powers over the malignant spirits which cause sickness. All maladies are believed to be caused by the touch of some demon who wishes to carry off the soul of the sick man to the other world, and the Manang is the man who has power to charm or kill the evil spirit, and rescue the soul of the sick man from his cruel clutches. When called in to attend a patient, he in company with other medicine men go through a ceremony which, though agreeing in the main

(52)

points, differs in details according to the disease and to
the amount of fees paid.

The Manang always possesses a Lupong or medicine
box, generally made of bark-skin, which is filled with
charms, consisting of scraps of wood or bark, curiously
twisted roots, pebbles and fragments of quartz. These
charms are either inherited or revealed by the spirits in
dreams to their owners as possessing medicinal virtue.
One important and necessary charm is the Batu Ilau—
"stone of light"—a bit of quartz crystal which the
Manang looks into in order to see the soul, so as to be
able to catch it and bring it back to the body it has
left. It is believed by the Dyaks that in all serious
sicknesses the soul leaves the body and wanders about
at greater or less distance from it; if it can be caught
within a certain distance, before it has proceeded too
far on its journey to Hades, well and good; if not, the
patient dies. Whether the patient live or die, the
Manang is rewarded for his services. He makes sure
of this beforehand, and demands his fee before he undertakes the case.

The Manang never carries his own box of charms,
but the people who fetch him must carry it for him.
He arrives at the house of the sick man generally at
sunset, for he never performs in daylight unless the case
is very serious, and he is paid extra for doing so. It is
difficult and dangerous work, he says, to have any deal-
ings with the spirits in the daytime. Sitting down by
the patient, after some inquiries, he produces out of his
medicine box a boar's tusk or pebble or some other
charm and gently strokes the body with it. Then he

produces his Batu Ilau (Stone of Light), and gravely
looks into it to diagnose the character of the disease and
to see where the soul is, and to discover what is the
proper ceremony necessary for the case in question.
Generally there are several medicine men called in, and
the leader undertakes the preliminary examination, the
rest giving their assent.   There are many different
ceremonies resorted to in cases of illness, but the following is what is common to all Manang performances.

In the outside common verandah of the long Dyak
house a long-handled spear is fixed blade upwards and
a few leaves tied round it, and at its foot are placed the
medicine boxes of all the Witch Doctors who take part in
the ceremony.   This is called the Pagar Api—"fence
of fire".   Why it is called by this curious name is not
clear.   The Manangs all squat on the floor, and the
leader begins a long monotonous drawl, the rest either
singing with him, or joining in the choruses, or singing
antiphonally with him.   After a tiresome period of this
dull drawling, they stand up and march with slow and
solemn step round the Pagar Api.   The monotonous
chant sometimes slackens, sometimes quickens, as they
march round and round the whole night through, with
only one interval for food in the middle of the night.
The patient simply lies on his mat and listens.

Most of what is chanted is unintelligible, and consists
of meaningless sounds, it being supposed that what is
not understood by man is intelligible to the spirits.
But some parts of it, though expressed in very prolix
and ornate language, can be understood by the careful
listener.   The Witch Doctors call upon the sickness to be

off to the ends of the earth and return to the unseen
regions from whence it came, and they invoke the aid
of spirits, and of ancient worthies and unworthies down
to their own immediate ancestors, and spin the invocation out to a sufficient length to last till early morning.
Then they rush round the Pagar Api as hard as they
can, still singing together their incantation. One of
their number suddenly falls on the floor and remains
motionless. The others sit down round him. The
motionless Manang is covered over with a blanket, and
all wait while his spirit is supposed to hurry away to
the other world to find the wandering soul and bring it
back. Presently he revives, and looks vacantly round
like a man just waking out of sleep. Then he raises
his right hand, clenched as if holding something. That
hand contains the soul, and he proceeds to the patient
and solemnly returns it to the body of the sick man
through the crown of the head, muttering at the same
time some words of incantation. This "catching of the
soul" (*nangkap samengat*) is the great end to which all
that has preceded leads up. One function remains to
complete the cure. A live fowl must be waved over
the patient, and as he does so, the leader of the Witch
Doctors sings a special invocation of great length. The
animal is afterwards killed as an offering to the spirits.

To qualify a man to take part in this mixed system
of symbolism and deceit, a form of initiative ceremony
is gone through by other Witch Doctors in the course
of which he is supposed to learn the secrets of his
mystic calling. The aspirant to the office of Witch
Doctor must first commit to memory a certain amount

of Dyak traditional lore to enable him to take part in
the incantations in company with other Manangs.   But
in addition to this, before he can accomplish the more
important parts, such as pretending to catch the soul
of a sick man, he must be publicly initiated by one or
more of the following ceremonies.

I. The first is called *Besudi*, which means " feeling,"
or " touching ".   The aspirant sits in the verandah of
the Dyak house, and a number of Witch Doctors walk
round him, singing incantations during the whole night.

This is supposed to endow him with the power to
touch and to feel the maladies of the body, and apply
the requisite cure.   It is the lowest grade of Manang,
and obtainable by the cheapest fees.

II. If a Manang wishes to attain a higher grade, he
goes through the second ceremony, which is called
Bekliti, or " opening ".   A whole night's incantation is
again gone through by the other Manangs, and in the
early morning the great function of initiation is carried
out.   The Witch Doctors lead the aspirant into an apartment curtained off from public gaze by large sheets of
native woven cloth.   There they assert they cut his
head open and take out his brains and wash and re-
store them.   This is to give him a clear mind to penetrate into the mysteries of disease and to circumvent
the wiles of the unseen spirits.   They insert gold-dust
into his eyes to give him keenness and strength of sight
so that he may be able to see the soul wherever it may
have wandered.   They plant barbed hooks into the
tips of his fingers to enable him to seize the soul and
hold it fast; and lastly, they pierce his heart with an

arrow to make him tender-hearted and full of sympathy with the sick and suffering. Needless to say, none of these things are done. A few symbolic actions representing them are all that are gone through. A cocoanut is placed on the head of the man and split open instead of the head itself, and so on. After this second ceremony, the man is a fully qualified Manang, competent to practise all parts of his deceitful craft.

III. There is however a third and highest grade which is attainable by the ambitious who have the means to make the outlay. They may become " Manang bangun, Manang enjun "—" Manangs waved upon, Manangs trampled upon ". As in other cases, this involves a whole night's ceremony in which many of the older Witch Doctors take part. They begin by walking round and round the aspirant to this high honour, and wave over him bunches of betel-nut blossom. This is the *bangun*, "the waving upon". Then in the middle of the verandah a large jar is placed, having a short ladder fastened on each side and connected at the top. At various intervals during the night, the Manangs leading the new candidate, march him up one ladder and down the other, but what this is supposed to symbolise is not clear. As a finish to this play at mysteries, the man lays himself flat on the floor, and the others walk over him and trample upon him. In some mysterious way this action is supposed to impart to him the supernatural power they themselves possess. This is the *enjun*, the "trampling upon". The fees necessary to obtain this highest grade among Witch Doctors are high, and therefore not many are able to afford it. One who has been through this ceremony will often be heard to boast that he is no ordinary spirit-controller or soul catcher, but something far superior, a " Manang bangun, Manang enjun ! "

Women as well as men may become Manangs. In former times all Witch Doctors on their initiation assumed female garb for the rest of their lives. But the practice is not common now, and it is only occasionally that such cases are met with.

Photo

G. R. Lambert & Co., Singapore

SEA-DYAK WOMEN

CHAPTER X.

THE Sea-Dyaks have no written language and have no sacred book to which we can refer to learn what their religious beliefs may be. They have no special forms of worship nor do they build temples in honour of their gods. And yet they certainly have a religion of their own. They believe in certain gods and spirits which are supposed to rule over different departments of life, and they have certain religious observances which may be classed as follows :—

(1) The killing and eating of fowls and pigs offered in sacrifice, of which a portion is set aside for the gods.

(2) The propitiation of gods and spirits by offerings of food.

(3) The use of omens.

(4) The singing of long incantations to the gods and spirits on certain occasions.

Sea-Dyak Gods.—The two principal gods or Petara believed in by the Dyaks are Pulang Gana and Singalang Burong.

Pulang Gana is the tutelary deity of the soil and presides over the rice farming. He is an important power in Dyak belief, and to him offerings and incantations are made at the Gawei Batu—the Stone Feast—which takes place before the farming operations begin. Should anything go wrong in the paddy fields, and the crops be in danger of destruction from any cause, his help is invoked.

Singalang Burong is the Sea-Dyak god of war and the guardian spirit of brave men. When Dyaks have obtained a human head, they make a great feast in his honour and invoke his presence. It is doubtful what the word " Singalang " means, but " Burong " means " Bird," and probably " Singalang Burong" means " Bird Chief". The Dyaks are great observers of omens, as has already been noticed in a former chapter, and among their omens the notes and flight of certain birds are most important. All these birds are supposed to be personifications and manifestations of the spirit sons-in-law of Singalang Burong, who has himself his counterpart in this world in the white and brown hawk which is known by his name.

Besides these two principal gods, there are numerous others of minor importance mentioned in their incantations.

Their whole conception of Petara is not an exalted one. They are spoken of as carnal gods delighting in food and drink as the Dyaks themselves do, and promises of food are made to them as a bribe to persuade them to do what is asked of them.

The Dyak gods, however, are good beings on the side of justice and right. The Petara can do no harm. Sickness is caused by evil spirits—*antu*—and when a person is ill, the Petara are appealed to and asked to help mankind to defeat the spirits. The ordeal of diving is an appeal to Petara to help the innocent and overthrow the guilty.

The gods and spirits are propitiated by the killing of fowls and pigs as well as by offerings of food. Long incantations are also made to the gods and spirits in which they are thanked for what they have done, and asked to help in the future. At all their feasts these offerings and incantations are made.

The Sea-Dyak belief in a future life has already been mentioned in the chapter on Burial Rites. But it is no gloomy Tartarus, nor is it a happy Elysium that lies before him. It is simply a prolongation of the present state of things in a new sphere. The dead are supposed to build houses, make paddy farms and go through all the drudgery of a labouring life in that other world. As they were able to help one another in life, so it is after death. The living can assist the dead with food and other necessaries, and the dead can be equally generous, and bestow upon the living medicines of magical virtue, and charms of all kinds to help them in their work on earth.

But this future life does not in the mind of the Dyak mean immortality. Death is still the final and inevitable destiny of man. He may live many lives in different spheres—he may die as often as seven times—but in the end he becomes annihilated and absorbed into air or earth or certain jungle plants.

To sum up then, the Sea-Dyak worships his gods, he has good spirits to help him, and omens to encourage or warn him. The traditions of his ancestors, handed down by word of mouth from generation to generation, are his authority for his beliefs. He makes sacrifices to them, and invokes the help of the gods and spirits in long incantations made by the Witch Doctors when called in to attend the sick, or on the occasion of their feasts. He believes he has a soul which after death will live in another world a future life differing little from his existence in the flesh.

PRACTISING EXERCISES, KUCHING

CHAPTER XI.

MISSIONARY WORK AMONGST THE DYAKS.

MISSIONARY enterprise in Sarawak commenced in the year 1848, with the arrival of the Rev. F. T. McDougall, afterwards the first Bishop of the Diocese that included the territory of Sarawak. At Kuching, the capital of the country that had already been fostered for seven years by the beneficent rule of the great Rajah James Brooke, the foundations of an organised mission were laid, in the building of mission house, church and school, and in the gathering together of Dyak and Chinese children, who in those unsettled times were brought within his reach, to be trained up as Christians. Some three years later, the coming of the Rev. Walter Chambers (afterwards Bishop McDougall's successor in the diocese) led to the establishment of the first mission station amongst the Sea-Dyaks, on the Banting tributary of the Batang Lupar River. At Lundu too, a mission was started under the Rev. W. H. Gomes, who, after long and devoted service in Sarawak, was afterwards called to take charge of the mission in Singapore, whence he passed to his rest after fifty years of faithful work in the mission field. His son, the Rev. Edwin H. Gomes, worked in Sarawak from 1886 to 1903. At Quop, some ten miles across country from Kuching, the mission to the Land-Dyaks was started, and there, as at Banting and Lundu, a substantial church of iron-wood (*bilian*) was erected.   Stations were afterwards formed on the Undup and Skerang branches of the Batang Lupar, and on the Krian River, where the station most distant from Kuching has, after a most promising start under the Rev. John Perham, languished for many years for want of a resident missionary.

Although Sarawak can boast of her roll of faithful witnesses, it must be admitted that apparent results fall far short of what might reasonably have been expected of over half a century of missionary work. Here and there, at times, wonderful progress has rewarded the efforts of the missionary.   But discouragement, due to isolation that could not be relieved sufficiently under the existing condition of the mission, either by sending men "two and two," or by frequent visitation, or by periodical reunions, has in many cases led to failure or the resignation of men who have found the strain too much for them.   Yet for all this, the amount of success attained supplies ample grounds for confidence that, given the requisite number of devoted and prayerful men, and the funds and organisation to help them in the best way, the Church would rapidly gain adherents in all directions amongst these children of the jungle and river.

The most striking advance of late years has been amongst the Saribas Dyaks, formerly one of the piratical tribes who were brought into order by Sir James Brooke, aided by Sir Harry Keppel.   While but few of the people covering the wide basin of the

Saribas River have been inside a school, large numbers of them can read and write their language in the Roman character that has been supplied to them by the mission press. Frequently it happens that, when parties of them go into the jungle for any length of time to search for gutta, one of a party who has learnt to read a little, will spend his evenings teaching his companions, by the aid of simple reading books that they have obtained from the mission. And at the close of their expedition, they will report themselves to the missionary who supplied them with the books, to show him what progress they have made, and to buy the Gospel in Dyak, and Prayer-books. There is one village in the Saribas district that used to boast that even its women could read and write. While visiting a village on the Paku tributary, I once witnessed the arrival of the local post. A stalwart Dyak entered the house with the usual salutation, and handed to the chief an old copy of the *Graphic*, rolled up and tied with string. The chief opened it, and taking two or three open letters from between the leaves, handed them to the persons to whom they were addressed. This chief was afterwards appointed catechist on the Paku, and wrote thus in 1907 : " In February we went up country with Mr. Howell, and I rejoiced much to see how great an advance the Church has made in the Paku River. There are now seven chapels on this tributary." To give this progress its due significance I must add (*a*) that two years before, when I visited that district I found but two chapels there, and (*b*) that the Dyaks build their own little chapels without help from the mission. Moreover, there is but one catechist in this division of the district, that includes some twenty villages, and no European missionary, up to the present, has been stationed in the district of the Saribas; a priest in charge of some other district going through when it is found possible. That converts should be numbered by scores in the year, under such conditions, is sufficient ground for confidence, that wonderful results would here reward the labours of a European missionary, having under his direction a staff of trained native workers.

The mission staff in the diocese has been considerably strengthened in recent years, but is not strong enough yet to supply all the stations that were formerly manned by European missionaries. The S.P.G. has grandly supported advance by providing for new missionaries as they come, and the Borneo Mission Association has done much in the way of providing means for restoration and expansion. But there is not yet a missionary in sight for the Saribas. But what has been accomplished recently encourages us to think that our prayers will soon be answered by the advent of devoted men to build up all the waste places of Sarawak, and to respond to the insistent call of the Saribas.

Passing on to the south-east, we come upon the great Batang Lupar River, the upper waters of which are as yet untouched by missionary enterprise. For some years, the inhabitants have been a source of trouble. But there is news at last, that they have tendered their submission; so, we may in future con-

Photo

GROUP OF SEA-DYAKS

Edwards, Littlehampton

sider them open to teaching. The Skerang Dyaks, on the Skerang branch of this river, have responded but little, as yet, to the Gospel appeal. A fairly promising start was made, with the opening of a station on the river bank. But there has been no resident priest there for some years, and most of the people have lapsed into the old custom. One Dyak catechist and his family hold on, waiting year after year in the hope that a priest may be sent to them. They keep the church and mission property in excellent order, encouraged by an occasional visit from a priest in the next district, and worship in their little church; a pathetic little group, standing alone amongst a people who will have none of their witness to the faith; waiting for the man or men, who will surely come some day to relieve their lonely watch, and order their advance.

Lower down, the Undup branch gives its name alike to a tribe and to the missionary district that includes it. This has been faithfully served by a resident missionary for many years, and has its Christian villages, and two travelling catechists. But the Undups, on the whole, have proved the least accessible to Christian teaching, and have severely tested the perseverance of their missionaries, who for all these years have continued visiting them, laying siege to hearts encased in a shell of superstition that for a long time, with comparatively few exceptions, defied all their efforts to break through it. Yet, going through this wide tract of jungle, one comes here and there upon a Christian village, with its chapel; a little stronghold firmly held, reminding one that the advance is going on, and that now here, and now there, the people, after many years of apparently fruitless toil on the part of their teachers, are coming under the power of the love of God.

Yet lower down we come to the Banting district, named after the stream that, flowing from the uplands down to the junction with the main stream at Lingga, passes the Banting Hill with its fine church, its little school, and hospital, and mission house. Here I remember staying more than once with a missionary and his brave wife, a doctor, who for thirteen years devoted themselves to the needs of the 900 Dyaks, who live in their long houses, clustering around the base of the precipitous hill that was once their stronghold, from which they bravely repelled the onslaughts of piratical hordes, in the cruel old days. Banting, once so promising a station, has been much injured in the past by reason of the weakness of the mission, and is now again without missionary or doctor. The pastoral work that needs to be done here, will alone tax the powers of a missionary, who must care also for his school, and the patients who come from far around for medical help. Below Banting Hill, and also far up in the country of jungle-clad hills and clear streams, are many villages that as yet, with two or three exceptions, are not being visited, and would provide more than ample work for a second missionary living at Banting. Yet lower down towards the sea, there are scattered groups of Lingga or Sebuyau Dyaks, easy of approach, and including a few who, in other places, have been baptised, or, at least, instructed to a certain extent. If these could be regularly visited, they should supply many willing converts, if one may judge by experience amongst men of their tribes in other parts. The Sebuyaus are said to have once occupied a district between the Saribas and Skerang tribes, who eventually compelled them to leave their country. They settled at the mouth of the Batang Lupar, in Sebuyau, which received its name from them. Large numbers spread into the neighbouring rivers and creeks towards the west, and their descendants are found in the Sadong River, in the Sampun and Moyan —two small rivers farther west—in the Samarahan, in the Quop River and its tributaries; and farther west still, in the Lundu River, where dwelt the loyal and brave Orang Kaya Temunggang, of Sir James Brooke's days, maintaining an obstinate resistance to his relentless foes, the Saribas pirates. Lundu, too, has fallen upon sad times. An excellent position was found for the large church and mission house at Stunggang, where was a large settlement of the Sebuyaus. But Dyak houses are not built to last more than seven or eight years; and, when the time comes to build anew, the Dyaks frequently decide to change their location. So it came about that, after a few years, most of the Sebuyaus moved away from Stunggang. This added to the difficulty of the work, although it was still possible to follow them up. But there came a time when their pastor was old and unable, in his latter years, to seek them out as formerly; and on his death, the district was left without a priest for a time. The people became lax and indifferent,

and responded very little to efforts that were from
time to time made to arouse them. With the coming
of a missionary in 1914 a new and hopeful era opened,
and there is reason to believe that Lundu will regain
all its old vigour in his capable hands.

At the head of the Quop River is the Christian Land-
Dyak village of that name. The people are staunch
and maintain their church well, and out of their offerings provide for their sick. I remember in 1910, one
outlying village with a resident catechist, who kept a
small day school going and taught the people as he
had opportunity, in and out of their little chapel. A
heroic and devoted Chinese priest, over seventy years
of age, managed to hold this centre strongly for several
years, walking out eight miles every fortnight to cele-
brate the Holy Communion, and with the aid of a
native teacher, keeping the church, house, and grounds
in Quop in most perfect order. It was pathetic to
read in his reports that he was physically incapable of
pushing the advance that only waited for the coming
of an English priest. His prayers and devoted work
bear fruit to-day in the fine progress that is being
made under the English priest who settled there with
his wife in 1915.

The people at Ta-i, Sentah, and other places in the
Land-Dyak Mission that centres at Quop are showing
much eagerness to be taught. Schools are being
opened in two places, and if the numbers are well
maintained, teachers must be sought for other villages
that are asking for them. It is always well to proceed
cautiously, for the Dyak lad often proves inconstant

ST. JOHN'S CHURCH, MERDANG, APPROACHING COMPLETION

when the novelty has worn off, and his parents will rarely put any sort of compulsion upon him.

From these, and an abundance of other incidents testifying to their desire to be taught, it is evident that the slow progress of the mission in past days is by no means to be attributed only to the reluctance of the Dyaks generally. Thirteen years of work amongst these people have convinced me that the harvest in Sarawak will be a rich one when the labourers are sufficient to cope with it. To one journeying through its half-starved missionary districts, its deserted stations (deserted, indeed, but for the visits of men who have more than enough to do in their own districts), its cheering oases where, under difficult conditions, the Gospel light is spreading, through the efforts of men little trained for the work; it presents the aspect of a harvest field deserted by most of the reapers in the midst of the reaping; left to be the sport of autumn wind and rain. Where there are reapers, the harvest is being slowly gathered in; and, thank God, their numbers are increasing. But they cannot be everywhere, and where they are not, the ears once reaped lie rotting on the ground.

It is not proposed here to discuss the missionary problems which must be faced. But to convince my readers that there are good grounds for the hopes I have expressed for the Dyaks, I will give a brief sketch of the progress made in past years by Sebuyau Dyaks, for the most part without any special training beyond that which the missionary might attempt to give them when occasionally visiting them, and directing their efforts.

In 1898, there was attached to the missionary district of Kuching but one reputed Christian village, which was situated on the Merdang tributary of the Quop River, and could be approached only by water, as in the case of most Dyak villages, placed, as they generally are, at the head of small tributaries or near the bank of the main stream.   Merdang St. John, as we named it, consisted of some thirteen households, of which the greater number were Christian.   On the occasion of my first visit there, a deputation of Dyaks came from Merdang Gayam, two miles up river, and made it clear to me that there were several baptised persons in their village, most of whom had lapsed. They begged that we would visit and teach them. Having little time to spend outside Kuching, I asked the young reader at Merdang St. John if he would visit them once a week.   He had had no special training, but had been for five years in the school at Kuching, and had been made reader because he alone in the village was able to read well enough, and moreover, had always borne an excellent reputation.   He readily undertook this voluntary work, and soon afterwards was teaching one evening a week also at Sungei Lumut, above Merdang Gayam.   Next came a petition from another village farther north, called Sabaior, where this reader, Buda, eventually undertook to teach for two or three nights in each fortnight.   At this period, seeing that he was giving half his days to missionary work, and was making good headway with the people, he was appointed catechist, and from that time onwards devoted himself entirely to the work of the mission.

THE RACING CREW, ST. JOHN'S SCHOOL, MERDANG

In Sabaior the chief, Laga, who sent for us, was a "manang" or medicine man, one of the class which, trading on the superstitions of the people, opposes the greatest obstacles to the advance of the Gospel. After our visit he became an earnest learner, and with occasional help from Buda, taught himself to read in the Roman character in order to study the Scriptures and help his people. And at last, having openly renounced his former practices and professed his faith in Christ, he was received into the Church, together with most of the people of his village, whom he had brought on. He continued to study as he was able, and afterwards became a teacher or catechist, and now holds his village well together as a Christian village, and takes care of another two miles away, where the people are now Christians. Besides this, he regularly visited Potong, on the Samarahan River, two hours away by river, jungle and swamp, where some thirty-five of the people have become Christians. Occasionally he used to travel for two days up the Samarahan, where he gradually obtained a footing in three villages. But he was old, and often unable to undertake the rough journeys; and the same may be said for Jalil, who associated himself with him as a voluntary helper in his travelling and teaching. Considering how little of any sort of training these men had received, one cannot reasonably expect that they could do much more than keep and confirm those whom they had won.

In the meantime Buda and his people at Merdang, with such little help and encouragement as we could give them from time to time, and a grant of £15 from

5 *

S.P.C.K., had built a permanent church of iron-wood, where the daily offices are now said, and where not only Dyaks, but a steadily increasing body of Chinese Christians worshipped on Sundays.   With his brother Tunggan, trained partly at Kuching School and partly under himself, he managed to take services on Sundays in two other villages besides Merdang St. John ; and maintained a system of visiting in three villages that are mostly Christian, and two others in which he was patiently winning his way.   At one village, after three years, in which a large number of people had been receiving instruction, the people, although professing a desire to be baptised, had not sufficient faith to abandon their regard of omens or the propitiation of spirits, until one day the " manang " of the village was induced to lead the way, by himself renouncing those very practices that he had till then inculcated.   After two months it was found that the people had quickly followed his example, and rejoiced in their emancipation from the tyranny of fear which had overshadowed their lives and hampered all their actions.

Merdang St. John had then its school of Dyak boys, twenty-seven in number, out of whom the four eldest had been accepted to be trained as missionaries to their people.   At first, no grant could be obtained from the Government in support of this school, so impossible did it appear to rely upon Dyaks to conduct it. But the excellence of the work done, both in the school and on the farm and plantations belonging to it, at length overcame this prejudice and won a Government grant.   When I came home on furlough in 1907, there was in the school a young man named Sait, a Land-

Dyak, who came to us asking first to be educated, and wishing to pay expenses out of some money he had saved while employed in an office. After a year his savings were exhausted, but not his desire to learn. He had been instructed in the Faith and baptised, and desired only to become a missionary amongst his own people. He was then studying to this end, with the hope that provision would be made for special training by the time he should be ready for it. Another young man there, Inggol, an Undup Dyak, who used to go with us to Merdang when he was in the Kuching school, was found teaching the people where he lodged on the Moyan River, farther round the coast, and with such effect that, after joining forces with him, the catechists were able at length to present thirty-five people prepared for baptism. And in the meantime Inggol, with one or two young men whom he had influenced, had journeyed on to the next river, the Sampun, and there obtained converts in two villages. At Merdang he was then receiving such practical training as Buda could give him, there being as yet no school for the training of prospective native workers or clergy.

The school at Merdang has struggled on to this day through various vicissitudes. An epidemic of bacilliary dysentery seized on the school in 1910 and took a heavy toll of its young scholars in spite of all that medical science and the most efficient and devoted nursing could do. It never wholly recovered from the blow that this inflicted on the confidence of the people. It still does good work under Alang who took charge when Buda was sent to take over an important school-enterprise at Ta-i. But as so many villages do in turn, Merdang as a village is disappearing, and the work so long associated with the name of Merdang St. John, may have to be removed, church, school and all, to a more populous centre.

When I returned in 1908 to Sarawak to find myself one of two European missionaries in all Sarawak, and without a bishop, discouragement at the depressed condition of the mission had robbed us of two of these promising young men. But the other two have come on and become very efficient teachers. But with a training school for native workers, we ought to have been able to secure and train several likely young men.

The founding of such a divinity school should meet in time one of the greatest needs of the missions throughout the country. From every district in which the work is being pressed forward comes the same call for trained native teachers, who cannot be supplied. And however little prospect there may have been in the past that suitable scholars could be found for a training college, there is no doubt that earnest men can be found now, if we can provide for them. The present condition of the missions amongst the Dyaks that have been neglected, is saddening in the extreme, but it should not be surprising. With a band of devoted missionaries from home, and a training school for the much needed native teachers, there is every reason to believe that we should be well on the way to the fulfilment of the hopes of those who, for more than half a century with little enough of immediate results to encourage them, have given their prayers, their offerings and their labour for Sarawak.

APPENDIX.

SINCE the issue of the first edition of this book several changes have taken place. The diocese of Labuan and Sarawak was founded in 1855, Dr. F. T. McDougall being the first bishop. In 1881 the title of the see was changed to Singapore, Labuan, and Sarawak; Singapore and the Straits Settlements being then included in the diocese. The Rev. G. F. Hose, who succeeded Bishop Chambers, was consecrated bishop of the see under its new title. Dr. Hose's episcopate lasted till 1908, when he resigned after twenty-seven years' strenuous work. In 1908 this vast diocese was divided, Singapore and the Straits being made into a new see, under the title of the diocese of Singapore, and the Rev. C. J. Ferguson-Davie, who had been an honorary S.P.G. missionary in the diocese of Lahore, became the first bishop. The Rev. W. R. Mounsey, who was one of the staff of All Hallows' Barking, E.C., was consecrated on the 25th of March, 1909, bishop of the original diocese, which reverted to its old title of Labuan and Sarawak, and Bishop Mounsey was compelled by ill-health to resign the see in 1916. During his episcopate the staff was greatly strengthened; and a great work of restoration and necessary building went vigorously forward. North Borneo greatly benefited by the coming of new missionaries to Kudat and Jesselton; and two to Sandakan after the retirement of the Rev. W. H. Elton just at the close of a long life of devoted service.

Table showing the number of workers in the diocese in past years:—

Year.	European Clergy.	Chinese Clergy.	European Laymen.	European Women Workers.
1859	7	0	0	
1869	8	1	1	
1879	7	1	2	
1889	11	2	1	
1909	3	2	2	8
1916	8	3	2	11

Up to 1889 the work of the diocese was confined to a portion of Sarawak. In that year British North Borneo was invaded.

The following stations are or have been occupied as mission centres :—

[1] Labuan, Kuching, [1] Banting, [1] Krian, [1] Lundu, Quop, [1] Saribas, [1] Skerang, Undup.

BRITISH NORTH BORNEO.

Jesselton, Kudat, Sandakan, [1] Native Mission.

The stations marked [1] are without any resident priest, European or native. Most of these can only be visited at rare intervals. Each of them has buildings and a roll of communicants.

In addition to the two priests who hope to go out after the war, we need fourteen new men: five priests and nine laymen. At an early date we should also have two more ladies to open a school in the jungle for girls. Given the funds and the workers we could start at once.

The financial aspect of the position is serious; we shall require for the passages and outfit of the above men £1050, and if they are to come on the S.P.G. terms at present in force, they will absorb an additional annual income of £2800.

The buildings which must be erected when the new men get to work will cost at least £2550.

For many years to come we must have a staff of European missionaries, for the Chinese and Dyaks are not sufficiently instructed to carry on the work without supervision.

An Association in connection with the diocese has been formed under the title of the Borneo Mission Association, the Secretary being the Rev. A. F. Sharp, St. Stephen's Vicarage, Thurlow Road, N.W. Since its inception in 1908, this Association, with an income averaging £1000, has done much to further the cause of Borneo at home, and has given invaluable assistance in the great work of reconstruction and necessary building expansion under Bishop Mounsey. The Association issues a quarterly paper, *The Borneo Mission Chronicle*.

BORNEO LITERATURE.

Life of Bishop McDougall.—By C. J. Bunyon. 2s. 6d. net. (S.P.G.)

An Early Victorian Heroine: Life of Mrs. McDougall.—By M. Bramston. 1s. 6d. (S.P.C.K.)

Sketches of Life at Sarawak.—By Mrs. McDougall.

Sea-Dyaks of Borneo.—By E. H. Gomes and the Rev. A. F. Sharp. 1s. net. (S.P.G.)

Story of Rajah Brooke. 1d. (S.P.G.)

Borneo: the Land of River and Palm.—By Eda Green. 2s. net, by post, 2s. 5d. (S.P.G.)

Historical Sketch of Borneo. 1d. (S.P.G.)

Picture Book of Borneo. 1d. (S.P.G.)

Seventeen Years Among the Sea-Dyaks of Borneo.—By E. H. Gomes. 16s. net. (Seeley.)

A History of Sarawak under its Two White Rajahs.—By S. Baring-Gould and C. A. Bampfylde. 15s. net. (Sotheran.)

Children of Borneo.—By E. H. Gomes. 1s. 6d. net. (Oliphant.)

Pagan Tribes of Borneo.—By C. Hose. 42s. net. (Macmillan.)

An Unreaped Harvest.—By W. H. Campbell. 4d. net. (S.P.G.)

Peeps at North Borneo.—By L. W. W. Gudgeon. 1s. 6d. net. (Black.)

The Doctor Bishop.—By R. B. Dawson. 1d. (Wells Gardner.)

My Life in Sarawak.—By H. H. The Ranee. 12s. 6d. (Methuen.)

———

The above books may be borrowed from the S.P.G. Library, 15 Tufton Street, S.W., 1, on payment of a small fee.

(1500/O.27945.)

ABERDEEN: THE UNIVERSITY PRESS